CHURCH &
COLLEGE
STUDENTS

CHURCH & COLLEGE STUDENTS

Why the local church needs to be at the heart of reaching university students and how you can be part of the story.

Miriam Swanson

Fusion Movement

Copyright 2022 by Miriam Swanson

All rights reserved. No part of this publication may be reproduced, stored in a retrieval system, or transmitted, in any form or by any means—electronic, mechanical, photocopying, recording, or otherwise—without prior written permission, except for brief quotations in critical reviews or articles.

Scripture quotations are taken from the Holy Bible, New International Version®, NIV® Copyright © 1973, 1978, 1984, 2011 by Biblica, Inc.™ Used by permission of Zondervan. All rights reserved worldwide. www.zondervan.com The "NIV" and "New International Version" are trademarks registered in the United States Patent and Trademark Office by Biblica, Inc.™ All rights reserved worldwide.

Printed in the United States of America

US Paperback ISBN: 978-1-62824-883-8
US uPDF ISBN: 978-1-62824-983-5

Cover layout by Strange Last Name
Page design and layout by PerfecType, Nashville, Tennessee

Swanson, Miriam.
  Church & college students : why the local church needs to be at the heart of reaching university students and how you can be part of the story / Miriam Swanson ; Fusion Movement. – Franklin, Tennessee : Seedbed Publishing, ©2022.

    pages ; cm

    ISBN: 9781628248838 (paperback)
    ISBN: 9781628249347 (pdf)
    OCLC: 1340973483

    1. Church work with college students. 2. College students--Religious life. 3. Discipling (Christianity).   I. Title. II. Fusion USA (Organization)

BV639.C6 S92 2022   229.24   2022944587

SEEDBED PUBLISHING
Franklin, Tennessee
seedbed.com

Contents

Foreword	vii
Introduction	3
Why Beginning at the Beginning Is Everything	
Chapter One: Why Church and Why Students	9
Laying the Foundation for Fruitful and Effective Student Ministry	
Chapter Two: Why Student Community	23
The First of the Four Building Blocks for Fruitful and Effective Student Ministry	
Chapter Three: Why Student Discipleship	37
The Second of the Four Building Blocks for Fruitful and Effective Student Ministry	
Chapter Four: Why Student Evangelism	51
The Third of Four Building Blocks for Fruitful and Effective Student Ministry	

CONTENTS

Chapter Five: Why Student Leaders   65
The Fourth and Final Building Block for Fruitful and Effective Student Ministry

Epilogue   79
The Beautiful Vision of Local Church Student Mission

Foreword

How I wished I had this book in my hands when I set out on the journey of church planting and student mission more than twenty-five years ago in the mid-1990s. I have known and worked alongside Miriam Swanson for half that time and witnessed God raise her up as a leader and spokesperson for this generation. Her communication gift shines through this book as she articulates the message and values of a kingdom movement that is much larger than Fusion and in which she and Fusion are fully invested.

With compelling argument and cultural insight, Miriam gently rouses the local church from her student mission slumber to an awakened, equipped, and alert posture. The student world needs something that only the church can give and a wide-awake church that can and must pioneer student awakening.

She sounds the alarm for both students and churches and gradually turns up the volume. I have no doubt God is speaking loud and clear through her words. Students need to leave today's universities with much more than a degree. A qualification is useful and valuable to both students and society; however, it does not come close to the value of knowing one's identity and purpose, and the wisdom to outwork that purpose.

There are other gifts that also must be handed out and received.

Students need to leave with kingdom values, ones that will never grow old and can be applied to neighbors and nations. Students need to leave with a vision that is greater than individual success and personal gain. Students need to leave with a daring and wild hope that stares down their own and society's struggles. Students need to leave with a conviction that they were born for a purpose, crafted, and curated in the heart of God. Students need to leave with their lives centered on Jesus.

FOREWORD

It is through the church that the gifts must be handed out and it is divine purpose that will be awakened in the student world as the church creatively and courageously comes alongside the campus. Miriam not only delves deeper into the why, she also very practically explores the how. She has condensed some of the valuable learning gained through the Fusion Movement that has now served and connected with more than 2,500 local churches of all shapes, styles, and sizes. The time is now, the alarm is sounding, the student world must be adopted by the church and this little orange book is designed to serve this most urgent of missions—that the local church declares hope in Jesus and home in his community for students.

Rich Wilson
Fusion Movement Leader

CHURCH & COLLEGE STUDENTS

Introduction

Why Beginning at the Beginning Is Everything

A young man walks onto campus, backpack slung across his shoulder, phone in hand. It's day one of his university career and he isn't sure where to go first. He's been given a schedule. He has a map. But now as he stands among the concrete buildings and unfamiliar faces, the journey doesn't seem so simple. He could really use a friend.

A young woman closes the door of her new room and flops onto her bed with a sigh. She's been working toward this moment for years. She's been looking forward to it all summer. But now that she's actually left home, school, church, and friends, the freedom feels a little more daunting than she'd expected. She needs a new home.

A second year student clicks "send" and closes his laptop screen. Across the city a bunch of friends reach into their pockets and pull out their buzzing phones. The group message reads, "Today we pray for the students arriving on our doorsteps. Tomorrow we give them the best welcome to our city and the campus that we can. Jesus loves students; let's go and show it! See you in the morning." The local church is ready to share hope and become home for their new student neighbors.

There is something uniquely daunting and exciting about the experience of starting college as a young adult. You might have in mind your own experience of this life transition or have family members or young people in your church going through it right now. You may already be acutely aware of the opportunities and challenges this season presents. You may be convinced of the need for young adults to find friends, community, and support at college, in order to thrive in their lives and their faith.

Alarmingly, choosing to follow Jesus at college and continuing a connection in the local church, even when raised in a Christian home or church youth group, is not a given. Whether you draw upon your personal experience or simply Google the latest research on what happens post-youth-group for young people's faith, it doesn't take long to discover the pressing need for a different story to emerge than we are currently seeing.

Too many students are beginning college without discipleship that prepares them for this life change, and without a connection to the local church. This unprepared and disconnected beginning can have a devastating effect on their entire lives. And that's just the young adults who are transitioning from church youth groups. For the thousands of young people starting college with no experience of faith or awareness of the good news of Jesus, what hope do they have? Who is available to welcome them on the campus? As they search for a place to belong, are there any communities of faith ready to welcome and embrace them?

It can be hard to know what to do in the face of such intimidating data or personal painful experiences, which can make you question whether going to college is a good idea at all for a person's faith or well-being. It can be overwhelming to know where to start with so many young adults yet to be reached.

So why does the local church need to be at the heart of reaching university students? The answer to this question has huge implications. The university mission field is a vast and vital one, but the fact that parachurch on-campus ministries, chaplaincies, and some on-campus chapels exist lead many to assume someone else is responsible. Why get involved as a local church too?

The majority of students are not finding faith on campuses and are not inundating our local church communities with new disciples. There is much more yet to be realized when it comes to young adult faith and the university years. So why should local churches get involved in this huge mission to students? Luke 10:2 screams the answer: "The harvest is plentiful, but the workers are few," and we must contend for a more hopeful and faith-filled story for the next generation than we are currently experiencing.

Imagine local churches having the tools and confidence to love, welcome, and disciple students as they start college life. What would change in this next generation if churches played their part in this story alongside those already at work in the student mission field? We hope these pages cause you to consider the university student mission story in fresh ways and to realize the vital role churches need to play in reaching this generation. We pray this is an idea that gets under your skin, that itches and irritates, that fuels prayer, deepens conviction, and leads you into action.

The university landscape is one that needs continual reaching and as such is the largest unreached people group on the planet. The story of local churches being at the heart of reaching the campus is only just beginning, merely scratching the surface of what is possible, and the need for this story to be written is increasing.

If by the end of these chapters you are not convinced that you are part of God's mission to students, and need to have concrete steps to move this vision forward, we have failed. Please read on as we explore why the story of church and students is one that must be told, beginning at the beginning, foundations first.

Why Church and Why Students

Laying the Foundation for Fruitful and Effective Student Ministry

We are hemorrhaging GenZ from churches at unprecedented speed. The studies and statistics are too familiar to us now to be casual about it. Many students and emerging adults are suffering profoundly in every dimension of life. If our church is in driving distance of a campus, we are positioned at the frontline of God's mission.
　　　　—David Thomas, senior advisor, New Room

CHURCH AND COLLEGE STUDENTS

Given the title of this book, it will come as no surprise that the model for student mission that we are advocating for is rooted in the local church. We want to dig down deep and establish firm foundations upon which fruitful and sustainable disciples can be developed. The foundation we are laying for student mission is the teachings of Jesus lived out in the community we call church.

We do not believe reaching the lost and making disciples should go around the local church, but that it should run all the way through the heart of what it means to be the church. We believe the local church is the primary place disciples can be made and nurtured and that this community of faith is vital for every generation to belong to, including university students. This may be easier said than done, but that is the story we want to tell, to invite you into, and where we will begin.

Who is my neighbor?

To begin this church-centric approach to reaching students, let us start by zoning in on the current picture to see just how close to home this story is for you. If you pull up a map online and search the name of your nearest university, you'll see a pin drop in the center of a bird's-eye view of the campus. The campus, whether a scattering of locations across an area, or one clear concentrated city-within-a-city, is in many ways a world of its own. Thousands of young adults live, work, socialize, eat, play, and study in this little patch of land surrounding the pin. They're right there!

Now search for churches nearby on that same map on which you've located the university. Do you see many new pins show up, probably with a cross emblem in them? Zoom out a little if you need to. How many church communities are just a few miles from the campus? How about your local church? How close to the college are your people located?

The thousands of students the campus represents are surrounded by praying communities of Christians—people committed to worshipping Jesus together and becoming more like him for the good of the world. But do any of the students know this? What would change if these communities prayed specifically for students? What if every church prayerfully and proactively decided to be and share good news with their student neighbors? And if you don't see a single church spring up for miles around, perhaps it's time to pray about church planting.

Looking at that map, with the campus, the churches, and all the young people's lives that it represents, it can be surprisingly easy to click out of the browser and pretend you haven't seen the need. It's really common for immediate deterring thoughts to arise like: *Those other churches are probably better placed than us to reach the students. We'll leave it to them.* Perhaps you're thinking, *We don't know anything about university culture, and we don't know where we'd even start.* Or even, *It's best to leave it up to the already established campus ministries to reach students, not us.* And so we as the church often click off the map, and hope that someone else, somewhere else, will reach students. We go on with church life, and pray disembodied prayers that one day, miraculously, young adults will somehow come flooding into our communities in search of Jesus.

Is that fair? No, maybe not. The chances are that you are aware of the opportunity and challenge of having university students nearby. But still, you may have disqualified yourself from being part of the mission to reach them. This is where we believe a different story is possible. We believe you, your church, your people, are just the kind of community that students need. We believe every student should have the opportunity to find their hope in Jesus and their home in the local church, and that home may indeed look like you and your community.

We believe the local church should be at the heart of making disciples, including the student world. And we believe making disciples of this generation of young adults should be at the heart of the local church. So, in Christ you are more than qualified to be good news for the campus. Students need the family of God and the family of God needs students.

Becoming a church with students

Becoming a local church that welcomes and disciples university students happens in big and small ways, over weeks, months, and years. Although it is tempting to jump straight to the how-tos of starting student work, we are going to stay with the *why* for a little longer. If you and your church don't have prayerful conviction that university students should be part of your vision for being the church and sharing the gospel in your locality, then no amount of action points are going to get you inspired. The heart for student mission has to come from God, and then the costly work of making student disciples will be a fruitful and joy-filled journey.

Why Jesus is really good news for students

College students are making choices and exploring ideas and experiences beyond the confines of their family home and upbringing. Like all of us, students want to live in freedom and want fullness out of life. They want life to feel purposeful, meaningful, and worthwhile. We know true freedom is found in Jesus and that his power and presence in us is transformative. As students deconstruct and assemble their new lives as young adults, Jesus himself can become the doctor, the gardener, the builder, and the author of who they are becoming. As students find their identity, the good news of Jesus can be the way for their steps, the truth which they can stand upon, and the life they can experience. This life in Christ is life in all its fullness, it lasts beyond this current reality, and for students it can start right now—if only they knew they were invited.

Why the church is good news for students

Like us, students need places and spaces in which they can belong—people with whom they can feel known, welcomed, and at home. You might think they are socially fulfilled at college with hundreds of peers at the same life stage surrounding them. But the reality is that many students don't find a place of belonging, especially on a busy campus. We know loneliness has been on the rise and now statistics point toward our younger generations being the loneliest of all.[1]

To be limited to a homogenous community drawn from a specific generation, institution, culture, and life stage can also feel quite stifling and is certainly not healthy for anyone. We all need friends of different ages, stages, backgrounds, and cultures to help us grow as whole disciples. We

---

1. See "The BBC Loneliness Experiment" for extensive data on this across nations and cultural contexts from 2020.

need one another in order to reflect the multicultural, integrated, intergenerational kingdom of God. Students find it refreshing and energizing to be around non-students. To leave the student dorm occasionally and be welcomed into a real family home is healthy for their well-being. To have friendships outside the intense student bubble, and to have the opportunity to receive input from people who may play a mentor-type role in their lives, is something many young adults crave. You may be surprised at how refreshing it is to be around young adults as well!

The local church is not confined to a certain life stage, but rather a lifeline through every season of our lives. We have a wonderful opportunity to teach and model an ecclesiology that introduces and establishes this firm foundation in students as they enter adulthood.

Why students are good news for the church

Student mission is not a one-way street. The strengthening and life that comes from young adults being full participants in the life of the local church is just as vital as the church's participation in the life of students. We need one another.

WHY CHURCH AND WHY STUDENTS

Students bring energy, cultural insight, ideas, leadership, and friends to the activity of the church. Those who follow Jesus already are often great inviters of their student community into small groups, socials, and Sundays. Many students are an example to the wider church, especially when it comes to evangelism and building community with new people. College can activate other student disciples in powerful new ways as young people embrace their own faith, some maybe for the first time.

If we are willing to create space and give them opportunity, students are some of your best preachers and worship leaders, hospitality hosts, and youth group volunteers. With their flexibility and availability during the week, mid-week social action projects, mentoring meet-ups, and online creative mission can all be innovated and delivered by the same students, who pull all-nighters or wear pajamas to do the shopping. They are remarkable wonders in creation!

However, some will still wonder if investing in students is worth it. After all, these young people might only be in a place for a few years before moving on again for jobs. They aren't often showing up with plenty of money and experience to invest in the church in return for the short time they are around. They can seem disorganized and difficult to rely upon. But the bigger question is: Can we really ask what reaching the next generation is worth?

Yes, *some* students may not be able to financially give to the church. Yes, *some* students may be called to a different place after graduation. And, yes, *some* students will show up completely inexperienced in church, faith, and lifestyle. We pray beyond the surface presentation many more are exploring a hunch that God is real and might actually like them. The other side of this story, however, is that students will surprise you. They can be some of the most generous, committed, and wise members of the church, and God is calling them to play their part.

The good news is that God has already set a convincing precedent for investing in messy young people. With only three to four years to work with, an unpredictable lifestyle, with no clear paid employment to sustain them by traditional means, Jesus decided discipling young people was worth the time and effort. It was the predominant strategy and focus of his ministry. Besides, Jesus didn't just pick the nice, smart, obedient Jewish boys who were already rabbis-in-training. He picked ones with tempers and ones with seemingly unrelated skill sets in fishing. He picked siblings, friends, and outsiders, and took them all on a journey of coming to faith and becoming a family. They were church. They were who then started and led the church. A band of misfit student-types, who were invited to belong to something (and in time, someone) as they learned, processed, and lived out their beliefs together. If it was worth it to the King of the universe, God himself, to serve and share life with a handful of beach-dwelling adolescents, then it's worth it for us to play our part in loving some of the thousands of young people at college.

Why student mission is really good news for society

> *"The university is a clear-cut fulcrum with which to move the world. Change the university and you change the world."*
>
> —*Dr. Charles Malik, former president of the United Nations General Assembly and Security Council*

CHURCH AND COLLEGE STUDENTS

Finally, if you aren't quite convinced of the importance of the role you and your church have to play in student mission, just think of who is in government right now. Think of who your most influential teacher was at school. Think of the editor who gives the final go-ahead to the articles and headlines you read in your go-to news source. Think of the last time you visited the doctor or the dentist. Think of the last bridge you drove over. Think of the last not-for-profit you donated to. Think of the big industries, corporations, and leadership of any nation, anywhere in the world.

All over the world, students are being trained and sent into every sphere of society. University graduates are likely to be involved in almost every industry and profession you can name. Running the finances, planning cities, building structures, creating resources, researching cures, directing companies, teaching kids, shaping the media, funding scholarships, and even leading our churches. If the fruit and privilege of getting to be part of the story of students discovering hope in Jesus and finding their home in the local church wasn't enough, these same students then go on to bear fruit in every area of society, in ways that will genuinely change the world and shape the future.

It would be good news if people who follow Jesus and are growing to be more like him were the ones creating policies, passing laws, and innovating just systems. It would be good news if disciples of Jesus were the ones reforming law, education, and business ethics. It would be good news if students who encountered the love of Jesus and were connected to his family were the ones creating art, music, and theater, leading in thought, word, and deed. It would be good news if we reached students from so many different nations that as they leave college to settle in other countries and continents, the gospel goes with them and keeps on spreading. Choosing to be a church who serves, loves, and cares about students goes far beyond campus, far beyond your community, and far beyond your reach. This sounds a lot like joining in with the great commission of Jesus.

Reflection:

- *Which universities or colleges are local to your church? What do you know about them and the students who study there?*

- *What has prevented you from engaging with students in the past or made you hesitant to invest more?*
- *What has stood out to you from what you've read so far?*

Action:

- *Create profiles for your local universities to help you hear God and understand his plan for them. Include information around their origin, history, and motto. Who are the current student population, where are they from, and what do they study?*
- *Spend some time thinking with God about your church community. What are the ways in which you could be a blessing to students? What are the ways in which God may use them to bless you?*

Why Student Community

The First of the Four Building Blocks for Fruitful and Effective Student Ministry

Our college ministry is large, but I'd say that our biggest fruit has come in the small. The most crucial part of our meetings is when we break down into small groups. It's where deep formation happens and where students can be truly known.

—Lauren Hansen, Young Adult Leader

CHURCH AND COLLEGE STUDENTS

In chapter 1 we laid the firm foundation for student mission: the bedrock of the local church. As we build upon this theological and practical foundation, there are four building blocks that will help local churches begin and grow fruitful and effective student ministry. Over the next four chapters we will explore the building blocks of student community, student discipleship, student evangelism, and student leadership. With these four blocks in place, we believe any local church can effectively play their part in God's big mission to students. Let's begin with *cultivating a student community*.

What if small is big?

Small has always been more highly prized and valued in the kingdom of God than in the world. God repeatedly seems to start small to get big things done. In Christ, we see God was pleased to humble himself to the fragility of a baby and physically start his saving mission to the world—small. The church landscape of the past is littered with awakenings that started small, often with ordinary people in intimate places of prayer and decision. In many cases these revival or awakening movements have begun with students, especially in the Western church context. The Holy Club formed by the Wesley brothers in 1729 during their university years in Oxford would later be seen as the root of Methodism, which also led to revival within the Church of England. The Haystack Prayer Meeting of 1806 in Massachusetts consisted of five students praying for the spiritual welfare of Asia and is seen as the seminal moment in developing American Protestant missions. The Cambridge Seven were a group of students who gave their lives to overseas missions in China in 1885 and this catalyzed hundreds more to do the same. We are hungry for another great awakening across this generation and we believe that obedience and faithfulness in the small will usher in the kingdom.

Why students need small groups

In the early church and life of Jesus, we see multiplication of small groups of community through intentional discipleship. Jesus gathered a small group of twelve young men who were on the whole-life discipleship journey with him. This journey included joining him when he spoke to larger crowds for more front-led teaching from the rabbi. Their calendar year was punctuated with a handful of annual festivals, which facilitated time to travel on pilgrimage together and also worship alongside hundreds, sometimes thousands of other Jews. There was a time and a place for big celebrations and these were highly valued. However, in the day-to-day and week-to-week life of Jesus and his friends, the small was where everything happened.

The vast majority of the life, teaching, signs, and wonders of Jesus and the way he made disciples happened in small groups. It was in intimate settings, around the meal table, in close proximity to those he was encountering, that Jesus chose to connect. Small groups were big contexts for the Son of God. Our challenge is: Can we be the kind of church that values these contexts too? Are we discipling students into this way of faith being normal or are they expecting us to entertain them as consumers from the front of a church building?

Students, like all of us, long for community: a place to call home, and a people to be known and loved by. Media representations of student culture might overemphasize the big party scene—crowded nightclubs, huge sporting events, packed lecture halls, and thousands on graduation day. But the fact is, most of student life happens in much smaller settings. Students live with a cluster of individuals, maybe a house of six, maybe a community of twelve, but certainly not hundreds. Tutorials and seminars also break down into the smaller, more relational structures necessary for real conversation, connection, and community. Even sports teams, theater productions, gaming groups, in fact, any university society you can name, create camaraderie and increase commitment through small groups of students with a shared passion and purpose.

Similarly, students who follow Jesus and students who might be open to discovering more about him are unlikely to feel they are known, can belong, and have a personal reason to stay and commit to a crowd. How can you ask your questions about faith in a front-led gathering? How can you recognize people and learn their names if you are facing in one direction looking at the backs of heads? If all of our efforts and resources as local churches are poured into impressive larger gatherings and programs, how might someone searching for life, community, and hope truly be seen, known, and even missed if they don't return?

CHURCH AND COLLEGE STUDENTS

Thinking about some of our attraction to and reliance on the crowd, this quote from a campus pastor rings true, "We do not go to church to get lost; we go to get found." Small groups are the setting where students can be found by Jesus and by other people. From this place of belonging they in turn can find others. In the vast sea of campus, below the faceless label of students, are individual sons and daughters with names, stories, scars, and victories, and they are worth taking the time to get to know.

Like Jesus, we and our churches must become interruptible to the individual and be able to stop, see, and connect with a person and not just promote a program. We can't afford to lose this generation by entertaining them in anonymous meetings while running the risk of missing who they really are and what Jesus is wanting to grow in them. This is the kind of God-in-people, incarnational encounter that can only happen when you look someone in the eye and know them by name. Small is big for the student who has been noticed, small is big for building community, and small is big for the presence and power of God.

Can small groups be both mission and discipleship?

Hopefully, you are convinced that to not have smaller contexts for students to connect to the life of your church community is to miss something vital in discipleship. But can small groups be impactful for those outside of the church and faith too? Can small groups embody the big mission of God to reach ever further outward to the ones yet to be found?

Again, let us reflect upon Jesus' original small group. This was his traveling mission team that learned, prayed, taught, healed, delivered, restored, questioned, ate, cried, fished, hiked, and sailed together. There wasn't a huge amount of separation between living life with Jesus in community and sharing Jesus with others as part of that community. Yes, there were moments of specific commissioning from Christ—the sending out of the twelve, the sending out of the seventy-two—but there were countless lives brought into the kingdom outside of these specific mission trip moments.

We can hardly separate discipleship from mission and evangelism throughout the gospel accounts. It all gets wrapped up in the whole life faith of being a disciple. Indeed the meaning of Jesus' call to "go and make disciples" (Matt. 28:19), which could be translated "*as you go*, make disciples," reflects this. To be a disciple is to make disciples and to find oneself being discipled in the very process as we go.

For many, small groups are becoming a vital place for inviting people to know more of Jesus, whether online or in person. Many students find smaller gatherings a safer context to explore faith and ask questions. For churches who have embraced the growing small vision—releasing many student leaders to host and facilitate student small groups—it is common for stories of salvation to bubble up out of these spaces. Roommates find themselves drawn into the little get-togethers happening in their living room and when students bravely invite their classmates and friends along to their mid-week church community. This is where evangelism, mission, and discipleship collide. When students share about their church small group on social media, other friends are able to join in too. Small groups are transformed into places of welcome for spiritual seekers and students are saved.

Christian students have a ready-made small group at their fingertips in the form of their roommates or sports team, their classmates, or society friends. It could even feel more natural to some to start their own small group with the support from their church with their preexisting social group, even if they start as the only believer in this mix.

We must not be overly concerned if a small group feels a little messy around defining where people are in their faith journey. After all, when exactly did Jesus' first small group of the twelve disciples actually become Christians? When they physically followed him? When they kept following him in the face of challenge? When Peter declared Jesus "the Christ"? Or was it after Jesus had risen from the dead? Perhaps when the Holy Spirit came at Pentecost? The important thing is to keep meeting and journeying together with Jesus as the focus.

Small groups can be dynamic places where so many elements of discipleship can be experienced. Eating together, praying for one another, taking turns to ask questions of Scripture, of our lives, of the culture, encountering the Holy Spirit, experimenting with different ways of focusing our worship, learning to speak up, to lead, to pray out loud, and to wrestle with doubt—can all happen in the small and committed context. Prioritizing student small groups will have a huge impact for you in becoming a thriving church with students.

Hearing this, there could be a temptation to designate your best and most mature leaders to be the ones to start new small groups for your young adults. Perhaps the dynamic descriptions of a thriving student small group automatically seem out of reach without either paid staff investment or highly experienced leaders taking the wheel. However, healthy and fruitful small groups where possible must be led by students for students. With the right support, training, and ongoing resourcing students will lead brilliantly. There are other ways to integrate generations throughout your church but if small groups are to multiply and spread like wildfire across the campus and into every pocket of student culture, students must be leading.

Growing small

One of the gifts of the small group model is that it is easy to replicate and adapt. What's more, if the group is healthy it will grow and multiply over time. Small groups keep flourishing because they stay small enough to adapt with their members and their mission. As small groups grow, it is vital they grow small. That means they must keep multiplying out so that students can continually participate in a group small enough to be known and to be missed, and to have a shared sense of responsibility for that community. The more small groups multiply, the more your students need to share leadership, raise new student leaders, and step up in responsibility to make new groups happen. The pipeline of helping to hosting, attending to facilitating, keeps on going as students are encouraged that there's always room to invite one more to the table. And if there are too many people? We build another table so that there's always more room again.

When small groups become a central focus and priority to the life and health of the local church, the overflow effect is that Sunday gatherings, and any bigger events you might try, actually become healthier too. Suddenly the crowd is less anonymous. New visitors have immediate pathways for deeper connection that they can plug into that same week. An invitation culture in the small will help an invitation culture in the big. Students are great inviters! If your students find hope in Jesus and home in the local church, and if they know there is plenty of space and opportunity for their friends to discover this, too, then that is good news worth sharing. And share it they will, in the small and authentic places of genuine belonging.

Reflection:

- *What is the place of small groups in your church? Do they have clearly defined vision and values? Do any of them serve a defined people group or gather around a common interest? Are the spiritually curious welcome?*
- *What pathways do you have in place to identify, train, and resource new small-group leaders?*

Action:

- *Identify three people within your church (whether staff or volunteers) who can help you think through what investing in student small groups could look like.*
- *Work through our training resource:* Small Groups, Big Mission *(see Fusion website)*
- *What are the main challenges for you as a church?*
- *What are the main opportunities?*
- *Who else needs to be a part of this conversation?*

Why Student Discipleship

The Second of the Four Building Blocks for Fruitful and Effective Student Ministry

Leading college students has taught me that my dinner table is among the most sacred things I can offer for the sake of the kingdom. College students are like the travelers we see in scripture. They are people passing through for a few years on their way to someplace else. When we welcome students to the table and to our lives, they stop being strangers and travelers and start becoming family. I have been surprised by the life-long blessing of loving people who are passing through.

—Jessica Avery, Executive Pastor, Arise Church

Who are we becoming?

When students tentatively take their first steps into adulthood, who they are becoming is dramatically shifted and shaped. The question is: Are we, as churches and leaders, ready to embrace this opportunity for student discipleship? Do we know how to help students actively cultivate faith that grows, takes root, and bears good fruit? What might it take for us, as the local church, to help students thrive in who they are becoming?

Jesus invited his earliest disciples to remain in him (John 15:4–5)—to grow and live a life inextricably joined to the life and presence of Christ. To be a disciple of Jesus is to remain in him, as his student, an apprentice to his life and ways. However, living this call and cultivating this kind of discipleship environment doesn't happen by accident. It takes intentionality to remain in close, transformative proximity to Jesus. It takes constant attention and deliberate action to create the kind of church community in which students can find themselves drawn ever closer to the life of Christ, becoming the fully formed disciples they are made to be. Beyond raising great volunteers, filling seats on Sunday, or even witnessing conversion moments, we need to create environments that position and shape our communities to bear lasting fruit. To do this we must consider our proximity to Jesus, our growth in becoming like Jesus, and our activity in being the hands and feet of Jesus.

Proximity

Being in close proximity to Jesus is transformative. Creating the kind of environment that consistently invites students to encounter the presence of Jesus is the fertile soil that will encourage their discipleship to flourish. Being near to Jesus means being close to his lovingkindness, his healing presence, his affirmation without having earned it, and his grace without having made the grade. This sets the tone for a disciple's journey and can transform a student's life if they can learn this in their most formative years. Just as Jesus himself heard the affirmation of the Father at his baptism (Matthew 3:16–17) before he performed any miracles or began any public ministry, so young adults learning to remain in the love of Jesus before they do anything to seemingly earn that love, is crucial to their discipleship. This is particularly significant in the results-driven culture we live in. At college, so many things are staking a claim on a student's identity. It is vital that the church is in this context, creating places and opportunities for students to hear what Jesus says about their identity.

Being near the presence of God leads to surrender. A student disciple learns that, in following Jesus, an ongoing dying-to-self takes place. We should anticipate a change from the way things were before students acknowledged Jesus as Lord. At times the church may have been tempted to soften the call of Jesus, to play down the sacrifice and surrender involved in following him in the hope of appealing to more young people. This rarely results in maturity. Students must be confronted with the challenge and cost of discipleship—to take up their cross and follow him (Matthew 16:24–25). The ways and demands of Christ make for a new way of living that because of proximity can be embraced with joy and lived out with passion.

Growth

Out of the intimacy of proximity with Jesus, disciples will grow to become like the one they are with. Students who are disciples often experience rapid growth in their faith and maturity during the intensity of their college years. This life stage lends itself to accelerated learning, change, and development, which is a real gift to the discipleship journey. Our hope and challenge as churches and leaders of students, is to cultivate their growth toward becoming more like Jesus in their character and lifestyle. Essentially, proximity to Jesus should cause growth in Jesus. This produces fruit, fruit that reflects the character of God and affects every area of the student's life.

In growing more like Jesus, we should be able to spot the habits and choices of students increasingly reflecting a Christlike culture. For example, that student who compulsively told lies to fit in may find themselves openly confessing when they don't know something or did something wrong, and choosing to take responsibility instead. The student who bit her nails down through anxiety in exam season may begin to wear nail polish as her fingernails grow stronger and prayer replaces her previous coping mechanism. The young man who had to be right in everything and was often the loudest voice in the room begins to submit to his peers, listen, and make space for the others in his small group, realizing he has much to learn too. The friend who invited their international student roommate to join their family for Christmas so they weren't alone on vacation speaks of a kindness that is cultivated through time and proximity to the generous presence of Jesus.

Students who are growing in becoming more like Jesus won't just have the right thinking and knowledge of the character of Christ, but they will have adopted practices in their daily lives that cultivate these characteristics. Over time they will be increasingly confident in echoing the apostle Paul by saying "imitate me" (1 Cor. 4:16) as they seek to imitate Christ.

Activity

One of the greatest gifts in working with university students is their capacity and energy to take action, to try things and to get involved. As students learn to be with Jesus, and then to grow in Jesus, we can also expect and encourage students to step out and do the kinds of things that Jesus did. One of the most rewarding elements of releasing and supporting student disciples is to see them step out in faith and experience the joy of God partnering with them in his mission to the world.

Jesus himself was quick to involve his earliest disciples in the hands-on action of declaring and displaying God's kingdom, up close and available. His disciples were the ones who physically fed the thousands on the hillside with a few loaves and fish. The miracle happened as the food was blessed, broken and shared, at the hands of Jesus' followers, not just Jesus (Matthew 14:13–21). Jesus sent out seventy-two disciples ahead of him into towns and villages to declare the kingdom of God, to heal the sick and to share meals and truth with those they encountered; no handholding from Jesus as they knocked on doors (Luke 10:1–24). The disciples did the baptizing (John 4:1–2); were in charge of the finances (John 13:29); were permanently on crowd control (Luke 8:42–45); and they even attempted to cast out some very stubborn demons and sought Jesus for coaching when they struggled to see freedom come (Mark 9:28–29). There was nothing about being Jesus' disciple that was purely academic or theoretical. The incarnation set the stage for everything; this faith was to be embodied, in the tangible, supernatural, skin-on, Spirit-filled reality of imitating Christ.

Student disciples must be activated to be and share good news. To do this, there must be space, opportunity, and support for living the kingdom life in the way we model church community. It might help to imagine with God what this could look like:

- Students praying for one another, for miraculous healing, provision, peace, and revelation.
- Students learning to trust God's abundance and live lives of generosity, even on a student budget.
- Students bold and unafraid sharing their faith with friends and neighbors.
- Students serious about justice and serving the poorest and making sacrifices that reflect this.
- Students who open their homes, friendship groups, and conversations to welcome the outsider, stranger, misfit, and searcher.

These are just some of the hallmarks of a disciple who is close to Jesus, is becoming like him, and is enacting the faith to which he calls us. What a sight to behold!

Creating a thriving student discipleship culture

We know discipleship is vital. We know that we want discipleship to flourish at the core of church communities. However, finding actionable next steps to move toward this culture with students can feel daunting.

The journey of becoming a disciple of Jesus is a living, growing, organic process. The discipleship life of others does not need micro-managing or excessive resources for it to develop. It should be a very natural process of transformation; one we are all made for. In organic farming, for a crop to be truly organic, it takes the right environment, conditions, nutrients, and attention to allow growth to be as natural as possible. Similarly, as we help grow student disciples, we can be confident that if the right conditions are in place, they will grow and multiply as God intended.

Here are three C's that can be implemented to help create, celebrate, and challenge a healthy discipleship culture among students:

1. **Create—make spaces for real connection**

    We all need spaces and places to connect with other people, and this is equally true for students. Jesus created significant settings to connect deeply with people in different ways. He had times of solitude and silence to connect with God the Father alone. He had times of needing his closest three friends to be with him, to confide in, and to pray with. He journeyed with twelve guys, his first disciples, doing all of life alongside this bigger group. He seemed to often welcome a few extras along for the ride, too, including a decent handful of female friends. He also spent plenty of time in crowds, at big dinner parties, and in full houses, where he would have connected with many more people whose names aren't recorded.

    These four social dynamics that Jesus experienced can be a helpful frame of reference when considering the ways students find connection and grow as disciples in your church: intimate (one-to-one); personal (two or three companions); small group (social but also personal); and public (Sundays, student nights, being part of something bigger together).

2. **Celebrate—tell the stories and keep casting the vision**

    Our words matter and what we choose to communicate speaks volumes, whether on social media, on the microphone, or on our website. To be a church that welcomes students and prioritizes discipleship in Jesus means that what we say, celebrate, and do all need to confirm this intention.

    What are the stories you choose to celebrate publicly? We celebrate the things we want to replicate. How often are you sharing testimonies of people in the church who are practicing a new spiritual discipline, or daring to try deep accountability, or beginning a prayer group with their classmates? What about small groups multiplying, students finding faith through friendships and hospitality?

If the discipleship journey means proximity to Jesus, growth in becoming like him, and activity in the world that displays more of the kingdom, then the stories we celebrate and want to replicate need to reflect these values. And who tells these stories? Having students on the microphone or on your social media platforms as the ones sharing their faith experiences speaks volumes about who you value and who has a voice and place in your church.

3. Challenge—do not give up in the cultivation and pruning of discipleship

When we look at the gospel accounts, none of us can accuse Jesus of going easy on his disciples and lowering the bar of the cost of discipleship. University students do not need more easy answers and spectator sports. Young adults don't need more consumerism, especially not in church. We must challenge students to grow up in faith and life, to accept the invitation to take a hold of all that Jesus is and has for them. We must be upfront about the cost of following Jesus, of dying to self as the gateway to true life. We must be unapologetic in championing a student disciple to live a life that is marked by the one they follow.

Jesus is clear that remaining in him not only means we will bear fruit, but that the Father will prune even the fruitful branches to help our health and growth (John 15:1–8). Pruning is challenging, healthy, and a vital part of everyone's discipleship journey. We want students to know that to be part of your church community means that together you will be pursuing the real and costly journey of becoming an enduring disciple of Jesus. This is an invitation that brings life to young adults, it is direct and honest, and it affirms that doing something hard and true with their lives is worth it.

Reflection:

- *What are the strengths and weaknesses of your current discipleship culture?*
- *What tools and pathways have you found useful to cultivate habits of becoming more like Jesus both*

personally and corporately? How are you celebrating the stories of this kind of growth with your community?
- *What opportunities already exist in your church community that activate disciples to do the things that Jesus did?*

Action:

- *Identify the tools you can pass on to students that will help them form spiritual disciplines in their own lives and friendship groups.*
- *Do a social media audit—what does your content say about your values and perspective as a church?*

Why Student Evangelism

The Third of Four Building Blocks for Fruitful and Effective Student Ministry

I went into student ministry because my life was impacted as a college student. I always wanted to win my generation to Christ, which led to desiring to see the next and next. This has given me hope that these will be the Christian leaders my children will be led by.

—Tharshish Johnson, Campus Missionary

The recipe for revival

There aren't many places left in Western society where people live, work, and socialize all in the same location. In historical revivals such as the First Great Awakening in the mid 1700s and the Welsh Revival at the start of the twentieth century, whole communities responded to the gospel and experienced incredible moves of God's Spirit. This was partly because these communities lived in proximity and so the good news spread fast.

University campuses are one of the few contexts within much of the Western world and urban centers across the globe where the ingredients for revival remain. In many cases, students move into the same geographical place where they live, study, work, and socialize for a number of years. When a move of God happens in a student dorm, the ripple effects of this are felt immediately across the student community. When a local church experiences an outpouring of the Holy Spirit in their college student group, it affects their friends, classmates, and even university professors. May we be the kinds of churches who send our people out in power igniting spiritual wildfires on the campus.

History tells us that many local, national, and international awakenings began when students were themselves awakened during their university years. The question is, does our vision for student evangelism go as big and audacious as revival or awakening, across the campus, and across our cities? And how could this vision serve to fuel our prayers, stoke our own fires of faith, and give us a bigger vision for what is possible through students? When it comes to student evangelism, there are so many day-to-day opportunities for the gospel that are almost unique to the student life-stage and should not be missed. Creating an evangelistic culture among students is part of being a disciple. It is vital for the life of faith, the health of the church, and the good of the campus and society.

The 24/7 opportunity

Living in a close knit 24/7 community means a student's life and witness is on display. Who a student is when they arrive home from a demanding day in lectures is seen and experienced by their friends, some of whom may have also been in class with them. Who a student is on a Thursday night out will be remembered the following morning by their roommates or sports team members because they're all still in the same community, night and day. Whether a student has a Bible by their bed, heads to a church gathering on Sunday, or hosts a small group in their dorm room, their life is scrutinized by the campus community. Students are sharing life and their behavior reveals their beliefs whether they like it or not.

This is a healthy challenge to discipleship. Living a dualistic lifestyle will be spotted quickly and so showing up to church as one person while being someone totally different in their residence halls isn't sustainable. However, living in community 24/7 also presents a unique opportunity to share Jesus and live out his way of discipleship consistently in the world. Every area of a student's life in Christ can be seen up close by their friends and becomes a powerful testimony of God at work in a person.

Do your students know and embrace the challenges and opportunities for evangelism that their life stage brings? How are our students equipped to pray with friends who don't know Jesus? Or read the Bible with someone for the first time? Or be able to explain some of their counterculturallifestyle choices with confidence and humility? Do your students know they don't have to be perfect or have all the answers to be a witness for Jesus?

The honesty of learning how to seek the ways of the kingdom during the university years, with all the mistakes, doubts, insecurities, and breakthroughs this brings, is the story of faith students must tell. The scandal of the gospel is the good news of Jesus and his saving grace available to the whole world, no exceptions, even on a student's worst day.

The remarkable effect of students who "get it"

The effect of a few students taking hold of the invitation of Jesus to be and share good news with their friends is a sight to behold. This kind of faith and activity is contagious in a community. Good news breeds good news; evangelism catalyzes more evangelism.

Have you ever had young adults in your community who have really embraced and embodied Jesus' call to make disciples? Have you ever had a prolific inviter or a natural includer and seen the difference they make? Have you ever had an evangelist who is thriving in the midst of your church community? If yes, you'll know what I am talking about. They can change a church culture very quickly.

When students show up to college excited to invite their new roommates to try church with them, whole houses of newly forming friends can end up connecting to Christian community. Students starting college say yes to invitations, gatherings, and new experiences to meet people. This is normal and positively encouraged so that people find their places of belonging. For students and churches ready to take hold of this openness to try new things, the offer of genuine loving community where the presence of God can be experienced is transformative.

Small groups of students led by students who "get" mission often end up having to multiply quickly to prevent them from becoming too big! Students have the capacity to cover residence halls, online platforms, cafés, and work spaces across campus and indeed the city, with these small collections of hungry people seeking Jesus. No need for big buildings, big overheads, or lots of permission slips and red tape to get through.

When you have students who love Jesus on campus, the church is present on campus and able to thrive. This is good news, this is possible, and we must not settle for student discipleship that does not make new disciples.

Why engaging in evangelism can meet resistance

Not every Christian student you meet is going to be desperate to share their faith with their friends. Not every student will embrace the witness of Jesus' followers either. We cannot be so naive in our talk of the wonderful power and possibilities of evangelism and neglect the resistance that will also be met when we try to mobilize our churches for mission.

Young adults have been raised with very different experiences and relationships with the church in regards to the concept of evangelism and mission. They are also living in a society where opinions and beliefs are becoming increasingly polarized, where people who see things differently from someone else are quickly marginalized or silenced. It is not an easy climate to speak up in and openly declare you believe truth is a person and a way to follow, not a fluid, subjective concept where "you do you" and "live your own truth" are the accepted answers to end a discussion.

In many places, Christian students are a tiny religious minority on campus and certainly feel like it. This is not necessarily a negative thing, but does challenge a student's sense of security and identity if they are the only believer in their peer group. Students can feel understandably fearful to speak up about their faith or offer an opinion formed by their discipleship that may come into conflict with the majority opinion in the room.

The fear of rejection is a powerful force that can prevent us from sharing what we believe. When working with students, we cannot assume they would engage more evangelistically if only they knew how. They will also need prayer, support, and faith-building stories to encourage them to share Jesus with others, despite their fears. If they are to live fruitfully in the long term, great compassion needs to be at the heart of the great commission. This will dispel duty and soften the sting of rejection.

Good news starts now, here's how...

1. **It starts with you**

    The most powerful teaching tool we have is our own life, story, and behavior. Even if you feel inadequate or out of practice, evangelism as a lifestyle starts with you, at home, among the people you know. It flows from the integrity of your own life so you won't be asking students to do anything you are not also trying to live.

2. **Change your language**

    We know how powerful words can be in shaping people's perspective. A really simple way to help create a culture where mission and evangelism are natural, expected, and celebrated in your church is through what you communicate from the very first time you meet a student. First impressions matter when a student comes into contact with your church community. If you welcome the student and say, "We hope you find all you need here to belong," that's good, but the church's welcome is focused on that individual student coming in and staying. However, if you welcome the student by saying, "We hope you find this community a place you can belong and a place that you feel comfortable enough to invite your friends. We'd love to meet them too and get to know you all," you've immediately communicated a culture of invitation and an expectation that church is not just for Christians. You have, from the start, taught the new student something more about being a disciple and being part of your church: we are also here for your friends.

3. Celebrate evangelism stories regularly

This is another opportunity to celebrate what you want to replicate, this time to create a culture for everyday evangelism. Whether in a coffee shop get-together, online, in a small group, or at a front-led gathering, encourage students to share testimonies of evangelism. These stories are a celebration of a student practicing making disciples, sharing their faith, or inviting their friends to know more about Jesus. A story that ends in life transformation and baptism is wonderful, but celebrating the shy student who plucked up the courage to pray with their lab partner is also a huge victory. In some ways, the more normal the stories are of sharing faith in everyday student life, the better. Keep reminding everyone: evangelism is what we do as disciples. It is possible, it can be natural, and rejection won't kill you. You'd be amazed at how God moves through our little acts of faith.

4. **Teach about mission and evangelism at the start of the academic year**

   As you welcome students to your city, your community, and the new opportunities their college life-stage affords, make mission central, not an afterthought in your teaching series and small-group focuses. Ensure the teaching is practical and not just theoretical. Season it with stories from your real life and the lives of your community, with tangible ways that sharing faith is being expressed. Be bold, clear, and invitational. Show them that student life is a perfect time to step into being a disciple full of light, distinctive like salt, on campus and for the sake of the world.

5. **Pray for students yet to know Jesus**

    How can you be intentional about praying for students who are not in church, who don't know Jesus, and who need to encounter the life, hope, and salvation he brings? Prayer-walks around student streets and across campuses are a powerful and tangible way to help your community pray specifically for the student population. All-night prayer and worship meetings dedicated to interceding for students provide a clear focus and often attract students themselves. Making space in church gatherings, large and small, to pray for the student generation keeps mission as a priority and our prayers from becoming too introspective.

Expect the unexpected

This chapter on student evangelism ends with an encouraging warning. Students sharing good news really can multiply fast. Expect to grow smaller groups of connection and discipleship as the reach outside your church grows. Expect to get your hands dirty serving the campus, cleaning up after parties, and spending nights in hospital rooms supporting students at their most vulnerable moments. Expect challenging questions, painful stories, supernatural experiences, and remarkable transformations.

Mission is messy. God's grace is so far-reaching that Jesus will attract, touch, heal, and help those who are not conditioned to church-appropriate behavior. Those who don't know how to fit into your current church structures will discover their place at God's table, too, with the help and welcome of your invitation. Enjoy the wild journey of student evangelism and expect, or dare we say, pray for, the unexpected fruit.

Reflection:

- *Can you identify any resistance in yourself and/or your church toward embracing a culture of evangelism? Where are these rooted?*

- *Imagine a week in the life of a Christian student in your church. Where are the opportunities for relationships with those who don't yet know Jesus? Where are the opportunities for connecting their friends with church? What can you be doing as a church to help facilitate the culture, capacity, and opportunities to serve this?*
- *Is there a current mission focus/culture in your church that could overflow into the student context?*

Action:

- *Who are the student evangelists in your community? If you don't have students, who are the evangelists in your community who you can draw into your student ministry development?*
- *If you could ask God for one thing to help empower you toward student mission, what would it be (e.g., faith for its impact, courage, opportunity)? Commit to praying regularly for this until there is breakthrough.*

Why Student Leaders

The Fourth and Final Building Block for Fruitful and Effective Student Ministry

It's important to raise college students up. They are the future leaders in community, business, ministry, government, and family—and faith is a key to that development. Watching students step into the fullness of who God has called them to be is incredible. Helping students hone their skills, and realize, walk in, and grow their spiritual gifts and God given talents is so powerful!
—Kyle Buthod, Director of Rooted,
College Ministry

The risk and reward of raising student leaders

Raising students as leaders, not just volunteers in your existing programs or planning, will be essential to sustaining your student community and creating its future. As student leaders' maturity and passion develop in their discipleship journey, they will in turn bring life and health to the whole church. It will be risky, challenging, and messy, but it will also bring a huge amount of energy, life, and fun.

The apostle Paul writes "Don't let anyone look down on you because you are young, but set an example for the believers in speech, in conduct, in love, in faith and in purity" (1 Tim. 4:12). The second half of Paul's encouragement is important if we are to understand that young people are not to be patronized, but can be culture-setters, disciplers, and teachers for the benefit of the whole church. Students can set an example for the rest of the community on how to live a life of faith.

It is certainly not just our job as leaders of students to stop others from looking down upon young adults. It is also about calling students higher into the example-setting and Christlike living that the apostle Paul sees is possible and deeply beneficial. That can and must look like leadership.

Raising leaders, not just volunteers

As with many of the aspects of discipleship discussed in these chapters, students may not be familiar with what it means to be a leader in a church context and may have never considered themselves as a potential candidate to serve in this way. One of the great privileges of raising students as leaders is introducing them to the idea that God may in fact be calling them to lead in some way. Through his Spirit and the support of community, this could be a reality for them.

The way we speak about leadership in our student communities and the way we model what it means to be a leader is important to get clear. Volunteers who serve existing programs, events, hospitality projects, and tasks which need to be delivered are vital. Service is such a fundamental characteristic of being a disciple of Jesus. It could be argued that every student in your community, whether they consider themselves a Christian or not, should have the opportunity to participate in the life of the church through serving. It is the way of Jesus, to serve.

Leaders never graduate from being servants. However, the language of leadership implies that people are following them or being directed and supported by them in some way. A leader inevitably carries more responsibility and has more influence to affect change. The call must not be taken lightly, either by those raising, or those being raised. Raising student leaders will always be a risky and messy task, simply because young adults are still being formed, still finding their place in the world, even while they are influencing and forming others.

Scripture gives us plenty of examples of leaders being raised imperfectly, with stumbling and failing along the way. Thankfully, God already knows the full extent of our weaknesses and still calls us to learn and lead with his blessing and authority. As a leader reading this, what do you remember from your early days of leadership responsibility? Would you release your younger self now? Remembering the grace and space given to us helps us look beyond some of the imperfections and obvious growth areas, to call young leaders confidently into greater maturity and purpose.

How do you start identifying and raising students into leadership?

When there is space and opportunity for students to participate and serve in the life of the student community and wider local church, identifying students with leadership gifting is straightforward. You and your team will need to know your students, their names, and their place within the community. Some students naturally display more obvious leadership characteristics. Perhaps they always bring a group of friends with them to your gatherings and it is clear the group is looking to them to show them the way. Others might be instinctively aware of who in the room might be feeling marginalized or out of place and you'll spot them making extra effort to walk across the room to welcome and befriend those on the edges. Another might be first in line to serve, even if they are last in line to speak, and their quiet presence clearly puts others at ease, even if they are not the most confident person from first impressions. All these insights and more will come from knowing, being among your students, and seeing how they operate within the community.

When you think you have spotted some leadership gifting and potential calling within a student, here are some top tips to begin the journey of discerning and raising them into a position of leadership.

1. **Talk to them!**

    Make an effort to chat more personally with a student in whom you're identifying leadership gifts. Getting to know them better is a vital first step. Asking questions about their lives, their upbringing, their faith journey, and their current experience of following Jesus at college will help you discern if their character matches up with their gifting. It doesn't matter how good a public speaker or how charismatic and popular a person is; if they do not display the fruit of the Holy Spirit or don't have clear signs of moving toward becoming more like Jesus, then this student is unlikely ready or mature enough to lead yet.

    A good conversation flows; this isn't an interview. Encourage them and call out the gifts of God you see in them. Be open by sharing some of your story and give them a chance to show they can listen and ask questions of you too. This is all part of building the kind of relationship you'll need in order to work with them in a team. If you are in a situation where you do not have team capacity to meet one-on-one, or if meeting one-on-one with the opposite sex is problematic in your context, then getting to know potential leaders can be done in groups of two to three students. Do not let feelings of stretched capacity or concerns around boundaries become blockages to releasing young people. There is always a healthy and wise way forward.

2. **Give them experiences of serving alongside an established leader**

    Releasing a potential student leader to serve alongside one of your current leaders is a practical way for them to learn the ropes of leadership. The existing leader is also sharpened and developed in their discernment and discipleship. Some ways of giving short-term responsibility without labeling students too soon as leaders, would be asking them to help lead their small group one week, or help deliver a mission project, or even create a series of posts about being a student and following Jesus on campus for their church social media.

Feedback makes all the difference, so give kind, specific encouragement to them as they step up in serving, including ways they could learn or do something differently next time. Let them know if you see potential in them to take on more leadership responsibility. Keep asking your team how they are experiencing this student as they lead alongside them.

3. Take some risks

The risks involved in raising student leaders take many forms. In some cases, the risk feels like the person themselves, not because of bad character but more as you try to cultivate space for a certain type of personality you might not be used to raising. Your risk could be having a highly introverted student as one half of the leadership pairing of a small group (there can be wonderful fruit from this quiet and unassuming way of leading). It could be risking giving a student responsibility as the point person for the first time, in ensuring a plan is delivered. It could be releasing faces and voices your church hasn't seen in more prominent roles before, be that young women, people from different heritages or nations than your church's majority, a student whose first language is not the same as your community's, or someone with a disability who may require more specific support for certain tasks.

There is also the risk of things not going as well as they could, at which point, as the one who is raising and supporting the student, it's you who gets to shoulder the criticism or clean up any mess caused. Behind the scenes you can walk through feedback with the student leader personally and pastorally, as they are still being raised and learning to fail along the way!

At some point you will have to give students real opportunity and responsibility, perhaps before either they or you feel fully ready. It is in the sink-or-swim moments that students often find their voice, their capacity, and where their convictions grow. Try not to feel threatened when that twenty-year-old's first attempt at preaching blows everyone away! There is much joy and deep works of grace to be found in risking yourself and your reputation on young adults trying things for the first time.

The students who lead outside the church

It is very easy to become church-centric in our discipleship and leadership vision. Even in the writing of this chapter, the language of raising student leaders has predominantly focused on what they can be supported and released into within the current church community. There is a good reason for this focus, particularly in the early stages of growing student work. We start with what we know and have: opportunities to serve and create within our existing contexts. That way, we can be more hands-on, give more away, and hopefully build up firm community foundations for other potential leaders in the process.

WHY STUDENT LEADERS

A culture of student leadership development will inevitably spill out of existing church roles and affect the leadership roles Christians have to play on campus and beyond. Again, this is less tidy and less able to be measured and controlled. Yet, it is also what we long for; that every student disciple would be able to step into opportunities to serve and lead in all areas of their life, on campus, future careers, and contexts.

If your students are truly called to leadership as they follow Christ, this should be evident in the way they hold responsibility on their sports team; in their class projects; in their part-time jobs; and in their presence with their roommates. If the church can learn how to raise student leaders who captain the football team or debating society with integrity, conviction, and compassion, then this bodes really well for their future and God's mission in the world. When they graduate into teaching in classrooms, creating culture in their families, chairing meetings, and leading initiatives in their places of work and life, they will benefit from the experience you have given them.

Raising sons and daughters

Although this chapter has used the language of leadership a lot, ultimately, all we have spoken of in leadership boils down to good discipleship again. We cannot raise someone to lead who is not first and foremost a disciple of Jesus. The best way to help a student grow in character and responsibility and to step into calling is once again found in helping them to become a devoted disciple, a son or daughter of the King.

Perhaps it is more helpful to have the picture of a family when it comes to your student work? Raising student leaders may be best described as raising sons and daughters to live a mature and thriving life in Christ. Like any healthy parent, as much as we may delight in the dependence of children upon us in their early years, ultimately we want our children to grow up, to become their own people: secure, whole, able to find their place in the world, not needing us anymore. We pray they always want us around for friendship, wisdom, and encouragement. But we don't raise kids to stay at home, reliant on us forever. We raise them to become mature in faith, embrace responsibility, and participate fully in kingdom life.

Reflection:

- *Have you released young adults into leadership before? What fruit have you seen from this? What concerns do you have?*
- *What does raising leaders look like in your church community at present? What are some of the encouragements and challenges you have taken from this chapter?*
- *How would you articulate in your own words the value and potential of investing in student leaders?*

Action:

- *Identify great mentors/encouragers/facilitators for student leaders within your church community.*
- *Identify vocational leaders within the wider church who can be available to help student leaders reach their full potential.*
- *Reflect on who has been instrumental in identifying, equipping, and releasing your leadership. How might you be that person for student leaders within your community?*

Epilogue

The Beautiful Vision of Local Church Student Mission

Over the last few chapters we have been exploring some questions—Why college students and the church? Why student community? Why student discipleship? Why student evangelism? and Why student leadership? We pray you now feel inspired and equipped to begin your next steps toward being a church passionate about student mission. This resource is only the beginning for what it means to make disciples in the student world and be the local church for the campus. We pray it has given you a taste for this kind of intergenerational church, a vision for the gift and contribution of young adults to the world, and a hunger for the wild adventure of sending disciples out of the building to be and share good news with those yet to know Jesus.

Ready, steady, grow

Ready?

May you know that Jesus really loves the local church and really loves students. He remains deeply committed to his people, his bride, becoming all she is made to be on earth as she will be in heaven. You may not feel ready to launch a full-scale plan of action for reaching the thousands on your local campus, but you are more ready than you think to take the next steps. The Holy Spirit lives in you, coaching, equipping, and filling you with the courage to go and make disciples, and to discover God at work in the student world. It could even start with you sharing this resource, and your initial hopes and prayers with a few trusted others, who just might get a taste for this adventure too.

Steady?

We have the hope of Jesus and the faithfulness of God as an anchor for our souls, firm and secure (Hebrews 6:13–20). Even in the storms of culture and tidal waves of change we are steady, inhabiting a place of peace and rest. This generation may feel light-years away from how you grew up or experienced adolescence. The college culture may seem alien territory, with no clear ways to see how your church could possibly have a place in this context. Young people might feel beyond reach, or disinterested, or distracted despite all of your best attempts to engage them. But we have this hope. We are anchored by Christ, the one who sets our feet on solid ground. As much as we might feel the storms shake our confidence, we will not fall.

Maybe the best gift you can give to students and the campus is to simply be the church who is consistent, who shows up, who loves anyway, come rain or shine, with hundreds of students or just three. Young adult life and student culture change so fast. The local church and the people who make it are in a unique place of being a steady, constant presence year upon year, to give hope to young people when they need anchoring and a place to call home the most.

Grow

We believe that the kingdom of God is like a tiny mustard seed (Mark 4:30–32). Although small in its beginnings and form, it can end up covering the whole garden with new shoots and roots of life. We believe that although student mission in the local church may be starting small in your church, your city, your nation, it is a kingdom work that will spread, take root, and change the landscape over time.

Let us not settle for quick feel-good moments of big front-led events and miss out on the hard won victories of creating small, deep, student-led communities of real relationships. Remember the mustard seed when you sit with your first two students praying for more to come. Remember the mustard seed when you have tens of small groups multiplied all over your city and you've lost track of who's joined. Either way, we believe kingdom work, by definition, will grow, often quietly, faithfully, and maybe even hidden for a while. But grow it will, into an astonishing harvest for which it will be easy, obvious, and a great joy to give Jesus all the glory.

Welcome to the student mission. We'll see you on the campus.

To connect with the Fusion movement further and to discover our resources, find us at fusionusa.us or explore the wider movement at fusionmovement.org

CPSIA information can be obtained
at www.ICGtesting.com
Printed in the USA
LVHW020249090922
727734LV00006B/15